DANCE NATION received its UK premiere at the Almeida Theatre, London, September 2018.

Playwrights Horizons, Inc., New York City, produced the World Premiere of DANCE NATION in 2018 with support from an award by the National Endowment of the Arts, and a generous gift from Scott M. Delman.

Special thanks to The Harold and Mimi Steinberg Trust for supporting new plays at Playwrights Horizons, and special thanks to the Time Warner Foundation for its leadership support of New Works Lab at Playwrights Horizons.

DANCE NATION was developed at the Perry-Mansfield New Works Festival, June 2015, with the Atlantic Theatre Company, and presented as part of the Contemporary American Voices Festival at Long Wharf Theatre, September 2016.

DANCE NATION was written, in part, in residence at SPACE on Ryder Farm, and received extensive workshop time and space as part of New Dramatists' Jerry A. Tishman Playwrights Creativity Fund.

US Production

Connie	Purva Bedi
Zuzu	Eboni Booth
Sofia	Camila Canó-Flaviá
Maeve	Ellen Maddow
Vanessa/The Moms	Christina Rouner
Dance Teacher Pat	Thomas Jay Ryan
Amina	Dina Shihabi
Ashlee	Lucy Taylor
Luke	Ikechukwu Ufomadu
Writer	Clare Barron
Director/Choreographer	Lee Sunday Evans
Scenic Designer	Arnulfo Maldonado
Costume Designer	Ásta Bennie Hostetter
Lighting Designer	Barbara Samuels
Sound Designer	Brandon Wolcott
Special Effects Consultant	Adam Bailey
Casting	Alaine Alldaffer, CSA
Production Stage Manager	Erin Gioia Albrecht
Assistant Stage Manager	Bryan Bauer
Assistant Director	Seonjae Kim

UK Production

Dance Teacher Pat	Brendan Cowell
Maeve	Nancy Crane
Amina	Karla Crome
The Moms / Vanessa	Miranda Foster
Sofia	Sarah Hadland
Ashlee	Kayla Meikle
Luke	Irfan Shamji
Connie	Manjinder Virk
Zuzu	Ria Zmitrowicz
Writer	Clare Barron
Director	Bijan Sheibani
Choreographer	Aline David
Set Designer	Samal Blak
Costume Designer	Moritz Junge
Lighting	Lee Curran
Sound and Composition	Marc Teitler
Casting	Amy Ball
Casting Assistant	Chandra Ruegg
Costume Supervisor	Claire Wardroper
Hair and Make-Up Designer	Giuseppe Cannas
Dialect Coach	Brett Tyne
Fight Director	Bret Yount
Resident Director	Hannah Joss
Company Stage Manager	Kate McDowell
Deputy Stage Manager	Surenee Chan Somchit
Assistant Stage Manager	Abi Cook

ALMEIDA
THEATRE

The Almeida Theatre makes brave new work that asks big questions: of plays, of theatre and of the world around us.

Whether new work or reinvigorated classics, the Almeida brings together the most exciting artists to take risks; to provoke, inspire and surprise our audiences.

Recent highlights include Rupert Goold's Olivier Award-winning production of *Ink* (transferred to the West End and transfers to Broadway in 2019), Robert Icke's productions of *Hamlet* (transferred to the West End and was broadcast on BBC TWO) and *Mary Stuart* (transferred to the West End and toured the UK) and Rebecca Frecknall's production of *Summer and Smoke* (which transfers to the West End in November 2018).

Other notable productions have included *American Psycho: a new musical thriller* (transferred to Broadway); *Chimerica* (won three Olivier Awards and transferred to the West End); *King Charles III* (won the Olivier Award for Best New Play and transferred to the West End and Broadway, toured the UK and Sydney, and was adapted into a BAFTA nominated TV drama); and *Oresteia* (transferred to the West End and won the Olivier Award for Best Director).

Matthew Needham and Patsy Ferran in *Summer and Smoke* by Tennessee Williams, directed by Rebecca Frecknall at the Almeida Theatre (2018). Photo by Marc Brenner.

Artistic Director **Rupert Goold**

Executive Director **Denise Wood**

Associate Directors **Robert Icke, Rebecca Frecknall**

almeida.co.uk
🐦 @AlmeidaTheatre
f /almeidatheatre
📷 @almeida_theatre

**LONDON THEATRE
OF THE YEAR 2018**
THE STAGE AWARDS

Principal Partner

ASPEN

Characters

DANCE TEACHER PAT	The head of the dance studio
AMINA	The star dancer
ZUZU	Always second best
CONNIE	A talented dancer who thinks she should play the role of Gandhi
LUKE	The only male dancer on the competition team
MAEVE	The oldest and least talented dancer on the team
SOFIA	Knows what's up
ASHLEE	Future president of a post-apocalyptic USA
VANESSA (aka THE CRUMPLED SAILOR)	Could've been a phenomenon
THE MOMS	Means well. Grown up Wendy

Note on casting, etc:

All characters except Dance Teacher Pat and The Moms are between the ages of 11 and 14 years old. However, they should be played by adult actors (for the most part) and should range in age from 12 to 75+. There is no need for any of the actors to resemble teenagers. (In fact, please *resist* this impulse!) And the more diverse the cast the better.

Think of it as a ghost play: the actors' older bodies are haunting these 13-year-olds characters. (We're getting to see who they grow up to be!) And these 13-year-old characters are haunted by the specters of what they will become. At times we should be fully in "13-year-old land" with all its ridiculousness, pain and pleasure. And at times we should be palpably aware of the actors' real ages and their distance from this moment in their lives.

The chants should be terrifying rituals that conjure real power.

The dances should take up time and space and be fully and gorgeously embodied performative events, even if the actors possess no real dance talent. (In fact, <u>*better*</u> if the actors possess no real dance talent.)

Cuteness is death. Pagan feral-ness and ferocity are key.

Everyone is nice.
Everyone is vulnerable.
And everyone is trying their hardest.

A slash (/) indicates interruption. And the character heading "ALL THE GIRLS" includes Luke.

1

Blinding white lights. Thirty little bodies dressed like sailors are tap dancing. They are flapping their feet and kicking their legs. They are perfectly in sync. Their faces are beaming. They live for this shit. It's the end of the number – they strike a pose.

Thunderous applause. A curtain drops.

THE GOD MIC
Alright girls. That's it. Good show. Let's clear the stage.

Thirty little bodies run in all directions.

A crumpled sailor is left behind. She is bleeding profusely and her femur is sticking out of her skin.

CRUMPLED SAILOR aka VANESSA
I can't get up

A tiny dancer dashes back across the stage without stopping.

CRUMPLED SAILOR aka VANESSA
I can't get up

Another tiny dancer comes back on stage. She sees the crumpled sailor and slowly backs off the way she came.

Suddenly, a voice from THE GOD MIC.

THE GOD MIC
Hey. You in the sailor suit. Let's go

CRUMPLED SAILOR aka VANESSA
I think there's something wrong with my knee

THE GOD MIC
Hey Minda? We've got a sailor down. Can you come get her off the stage please?

MINDA *(Yelling from somewhere far offstage.)*
Coming!!!!

A long moment of the crumpled sailor alone on the stage, bleeding.

One-by-one the tiny dancers come back on stage and stand in horror around the crumpled sailor.

SOFIA
Oh my god

MAEVE
Oh my god

ASHLEE
Oh my god! Vanessa! What happened?

CRUMPLED SAILOR aka VANESSA
I landed funny

MAEVE
Wow. That's really bad

One of THE GIRLS starts to cry.

THE GOD MIC
Hey Minda? Can you bring some paper towels? And maybe some–

MINDA *(Yelling from somewhere offstage.)*
Sorry! Just a minute!

CONNIE
Does it hurt?

One of the stage lights comes undone. It falls to the stage and lands with an enormous BANG like a cannon going off.

The tiny dancers scream and run in all directions.

The crumpled sailor – once again all alone onstage and bleeding. A long moment of silence, and then…

THE GOD MIC
Just sit tight, honey. Someone's calling an ambulance.

2

DANCE TEACHER PAT stands in front of an army of little girls and LUKE – the one male dancer in the group.

DANCE TEACHER PAT
Alright girls
We've got a lot of work to do
Nationals is a month away
And we're a mess.
Maeve. Get that hair out of your face

MAEVE pushes her hair back. It falls back into her eyes.

DANCE TEACHER PAT
Where's your hair tie?

MAEVE
In the dressing room

DANCE TEACHER PAT
Run and get it

MAEVE runs out of the studio to get a hair tie.

DANCE TEACHER PAT
Now we all get to wait for Maeve…

They wait for Maeve.

…
…
…
…
…
…

MAEVE comes running back, her bangs awkwardly pinned back with butterfly clips. DANCE TEACHER PAT clears his throat.

DANCE TEACHER PAT
Alright. Where was I?

MAEVE

...*sorry*

He holds up a thumb.

DANCE TEACHER PAT

This week? We're off to the Legacy National Talent
Competition in Philadelphia

He adds a finger.

DANCE TEACHER PAT

Next week? We take the bus to Akron, Ohio, for StarPower USA

And a third finger...

DANCE TEACHER PAT

Then it's Lanoka Harbor, New Jersey, for The Boogie Down
Grand Prix

He starts with his thumb again and counts up.

DANCE TEACHER PAT

If we win in Philadelphia...
If we win in Akron, Ohio...
And if we win in Lanoka Harbor, New Jersey, at The Boogie
Down Grand Prix
(And I'm talking Overall 1st Place finishes or nothing)
We will pack our bags...
And we will get on a plane...

And we will fly all the way to TAMPA BAY,
FLORIDAAAAAAAAAAAA

ALL THE GIRLS

Yes!
Yes!
Yesss!

DANCE TEACHER PAT

FOR NATIONALSSSSSSSSSSS

ALL THE GIRLS
Yes!
Yes!
Yesss!

DANCE TEACHER PAT

IN FLORIDAAAAAAAAAAAAAA

He silences them.

They hush.

DANCE TEACHER PAT
Now some of you are bumpin at the top of the pre-teen
division, and next year I'm gonna have to bump you up
to teens. (Connie. Ashlee. Zuzu. I'm talking to you.) You're
gonna be at the bottom of the pile again and you're gonna
have to crawl your way back to the top…

ALL THE GIRLS
…

DANCE TEACHER PAT
But right now you're Big Dogs…
How're you gonna cap off your prepubescent years?
Will you be winners?
Like the Elite Pre-Teen Competition Squad of 1992?

*He raps a framed photograph of The Elite Pre-Teen Competition
Squad of 1992. They are in sequins and face-paint and grasping a
4-foot-tall trophy – vicious, victorious.*

DANCE TEACHER PAT
Or '95

He raps another photo on the wall.

DANCE TEACHER PAT
Or '97

And another.

DANCE TEACHER PAT
Or two-thousand-thirteen. *Fourteen. Fifteen!*
Three years in a row
Boom, boom, boom
…
…
Or will you not even make it to The Wall…

ALL THE GIRLS
…

DANCE TEACHER PAT
Who were the girls in 1996?
We don't know….
It's like they never even existed

ALL THE GIRLS
…

DANCE TEACHER PAT
But the girls in 1997…………………
You remember who they were, don't you????

ALL THE GIRLS whisper, mesmerized by the memory of…

ALL THE GIRLS *(Whispering.)*
Sabinaaaaaaaaaaaaa

DANCE TEACHER PAT
Yes, Sabina

ALL THE GIRLS
Sabinaaaaaaaaaaaaaaaaaaa

THE GIRLS gaze admiringly at a portrait of Sabina – beautiful, gracious, wearing an enormous crown.

DANCE TEACHER PAT
It was at Nationals in West Bend, Wisconsin, nineteen years ago that Sabina Maratzi was first spotted by a casting agent from the Telsey & Company in New York City and six years later she was dancing in the chorus of a Broadway show

ALL THE GIRLS hiss like snakes.

ALL THE GIRLS
Sssssssssssssssssssssssssss

DANCE TEACHER PAT
Maybe it'll be one of *you* this time… Maybe this is the year, this is the moment, this is the dance where your lives will *start!*

ALL THE GIRLS
I want my life to start! Oh pleazz!

DANCE TEACHER PAT
Now we're shaking things up. We may have won with the sailors in Ashley, PA, but it's not gonna cut it for Philly

ALL THE GIRLS
…

DANCE TEACHER PAT
We need something different. Something *special.* Something these judges have never seen before. Something that's gonna kick 'em in the gut and tell 'em there's a revolution coming out of Harrington, Ohio! *THIS IS THE FUTURE! I AM MAKING THE FUTURE!! WE'RE GONNA MAKE THOSE JUDGES FEEL SOMETHING IN THEIR COLD, DEAD, PERNICIOUS HEARTS!!*

ALL THE GIRLS
!!!!

DANCE TEACHER PAT
It's going to be an acro-lyrical number

THE GIRLS all gasp.

DANCE TEACHER PAT
It's called WORLD ON FIRE and it's about the legacy of
Gandhi. Who can tell me who that is?

THE GIRLS and LUKE look at their feet.

CONNIE and AMINA tentatively raise their hands.

DANCE TEACHER PAT
Yes, Amina?

AMINA
He's a leader.

DANCE TEACHER PAT
He's from India.

DANCE TEACHER PAT looks at them, genuinely perplexed.

DANCE TEACHER PAT
Why don't you girls know this? He went on a hunger strike
and stopped eating.

DANCE TEACHER PAT looks at them menacingly.

DANCE TEACHER PAT
It's going to be a really beautiful number about resistance.
You'll all be playing Citizens of the World. And one of you
will play the role of Gandhi.

*They all look at CONNIE – the only Indian-American student in
the class. SOFIA raises her hand.*

DANCE TEACHER
Yes Sofia

SOFIA
I don't think it's fair that Gandhi is the star

They all look at CONNIE.

DANCE TEACHER
I don't know which one of you will play the role of Gandhi yet.
It could be anyone.

ZUZU raises her hand.

ZUZU
I'd really like to play the role of Gandhi.

DANCE TEACHER
You're all going to learn the part and then we'll see who does it best.

LUKE raises his hand.

DANCE TEACHER PAT
Yes Luke?

LUKE
Is Vanessa okay?

DANCE TEACHER
Vanessa's in the hospital. Vanessa's doing fine.

LUKE
Is she coming back?

DANCE TEACHER PAT
Vanessa won't be dancing with us for awhile.

They all look at the floor.

DANCE TEACHER PAT
That's what happens when you don't roll through your feet
properly when you land.
Alright. Spread apart!

THE GIRLS get into formation.

DANCE TEACHER PAT
I want you to learn it as if it's your solo to lose

3

Drumroll! THE GIRLS and LUKE audition for the part of Gandhi.

ASHLEE

I hope I get it!

They do the dance as if we could only see a close-up on their faces. They are perfectly still except for their eyebrows, their nostrils, their mouths, etc. and the occasional dramatic arm movement. At the moment in the dance where they would leap, they breathe in deeply through their nostrils. At the moment in the dance where they would do a series of turns, they breathe out through their mouths. They furrow their brows as the music swells and then break into a radiant look of surprise. Everything is perfectly choreographed. It is a complex and exquisitely rendered ballet of the face.

DANCE TEACHER PAT
Alright. Good stuff

THE GIRLS disperse. He calls after them...

DANCE TEACHER PAT
REMEMBER TO CLOSE YOUR MOUTH WHEN YOU TURN, ASHLEE! Everybody needs to work on their faces

He claps on each word.

DANCE TEACHER PAT
Sadness, Surprise, Fierce
Sadness, Surprise, Fierce
I want you to practice in front of the mirror
No limp arms, or I'll cut them off!

Almost ALL THE GIRLS are gone now. ZUZU catches up to AMINA.

ZUZU
Hey

AMINA
Hey

ZUZU
Good job!

AMINA
You, too!

ZUZU
You were awesome

AMINA
Oh my god. *You* were awesome

ZUZU
Your turns were crazy. You went so fast

AMINA
I loved your chest roll. You were so *intense*

ZUZU
Really?????

AMINA
You're such a diva

ZUZU
Was my side aerial okay?

AMINA
Yeah it was good

ZUZU
It felt a little lopsided

AMINA
Maybe a little but you caught it

ZUZU
But a little?

AMINA
Maybe a little but I didn't really notice, I feel like you pulled it off

ZUZU
Okay good

AMINA
What about mine?

ZUZU
It was perfect

AMINA
Are you sure?

ZUZU
It was totally perfect

AMINA
Okay cool

ZUZU
Your turns were perfect, too

AMINA
I'm always worried that I go too fast

ZUZU
No, / no it's cool

AMINA
And lose control. It's not good to lose control

ZUZU
I like it

They smile at each other.

AMINA
I hope we both just get it

ZUZU
Yeah! I hope we're both just Gandhi!

AMINA
OH MY GOD

ZUZU
What?!

AMINA
That would be *perfect!*

> *CONNIE's still there, drinking from her water bottle. She waves at them.*

CONNIE
Hey

4

The dressing room post-auditions. THE GIRLS are changing into their street clothes. They get completely, uninhibitedly butt-ass naked in front of each other as they talk. LUKE is separated from them by a little curtain.

ASHLEE
If I get a dog, it's gonna be a wolf dog

CONNIE *Sofi*
A what?

ASHLEE
A wolf dog

CONNIE
That's bad for the wolves

SOFIA
What's a wolf dog?

ASHLEE
No it's not

AMINA
Half-dog, half-wolf

CONNIE
Ask Maeve. She's really into wolf preservation

ASHLEE
Maeve

MAEVE
I'm really into what?

CONNIE
Wolf preservation

MAEVE
Oh. Yeah

ASHLEE
I wanna get a wolf dog

MAEVE
That's bad

CONNIE
See

ASHLEE
Why is that bad? / They're beautiful

MAEVE
It's bad for the wolves. They're not pets. / They're wild animals

SOFIA
I'm not into wolf preservation. I'm into wolf extinction

CONNIE	**ASHLEE**
Okay, you freak	Wait. Are you serious?

SOFIA
I'm not really into wolf extinction. I just think they're scary

ASHLEE
They're not scary

MAEVE
I want to walk to school with wolves

CONNIE
No you don't

MAEVE
Yes I do! I want to walk to school with the wolves howling / in the mountains

SOFIA
Hey Amina. Did you do it?

AMINA
Huh?

SOFIA makes a gesture like she's thwacking a pussy.

AMINA
I tried

SOFIA
You *tried?*

AMINA
Nothing happened

SOFIA
Nothing happened???!!

AMINA
I don't know why. I really tried!

SOFIA	**ASHLEE**
What did you do?	Wait. What's happening?

CONNIE *(To ASHLEE.)*
She's teaching Amina how to masturbate

SOFIA *(To CONNIE.)*
Shut up

ASHLEE	**CONNIE**
To masturbate?	What? I think it's cool!

SOFIA
Wait, so. What did you do?

AMINA
I don't know. I just did what you told me

SOFIA
Uh-huh

AMINA
For like a long time

SOFIA
What did you think about?

AMINA
You're supposed to think about something?

SOFIA
Amina! That's like–
The whole thing
Is mostly / just thinking

CONNIE
Yeah, it's mostly just thinking

AMINA
What do you think about?

SOFIA
I don't know I'll tell you later

CONNIE
Swimsuits

> *CONNIE laughs.*

CONNIE
I don't know why. I mostly think about like… *Luke???*

LUKE *(From behind the curtain.)*
Yeah?

CONNIE
Don't listen! …………………taking off swimsuits

ASHLEE
I mostly think about someone being really mad at me. And
pinning me to the ground. And like. Yelling

> *SOFIA pulls up her pants.*

SOFIA
My sister says there's this thing called your *pica*?

CONNIE
Uh-huh

SOFIA
And it's between your asshole and your privates

26

ASHLEE

Oh, wow

LUKE parts the curtain and joins THE GIRLS.

MAEVE

Hi Luke

ASHLEE

Hi Luke

LUKE

Hey

SOFIA

And it's where dance originated from. Like the first humans.
They all danced from their *pica*. Instead of their core.
Everything came from their *pica*.

MAEVE

I wish we got to dance from our *picas!*

ASHLEE

Where is it again?

SOFIA

The little stretch of land between your asshole and your privates…

ASHLEE

…

…

…

SOFIA *(Laughing.)*

What're you doing?!

ASHLEE

I'm just– Finding it

AMINA

Who do you guys think is going to be Gandhi?

27

MAEVE
You

LUKE
You

ASHLEE
It's always you

AMINA
Not always. Last time it was Maeve

SOFIA
That's just cuz Maeve makes the best sailor

MAEVE
ARGGG

AMINA
I don't know. I hope I'm not losing my spark

CONNIE
I think I should be Gandhi

ASHLEE
I think Connie should be Gandhi too

ALL THE GIRLS
…

CONNIE
I think it's weird if Amina's Gandhi
   (To AMINA.)
I think you don't really *fit*

SOFIA
I think anyone can play Gandhi because Gandhi was about
loving and accepting all people

CONNIE
…

LUKE
Maybe Zuzu will be Gandhi

SOFIA
Zuzu's not going to be Gandhi

LUKE
Why not?

SOFIA
Because she's not as good as Amina

LUKE
I think Zuzu would make a good Gandhi

CONNIE
Where's Zuzu?

ASHLEE
Where's Zuzu?

MAEVE
She's talking to her mom

    ZUZU just outside the dressing room, talking to her mom.

ZUZU'S MOM
Did you get intimidated?

ZUZU
No?

ZUZU'S MOM
It's intimidating, isn't it?

ZUZU

…

ZUZU'S MOM
You did great, honey

ZUZU

I know…

ZUZU'S MOM

You'll get it next time. Just don't psyche yourself out, okay?

ZUZU

I won't

ZUZU'S MOM

You're better than Amina. You just have to not psyche yourself out

ZUZU

I'm not psyching myself out

ZUZU'S MOM

She may be more technically skilled than you, you know, but it doesn't matter. It's the heart that matters, you know. She may be flawless but it doesn't matter because she doesn't dance with any *heart*, you know what I'm saying. You have heart. That's why she'll never really beat you even if she wins

ZUZU

I win sometimes

ZUZU'S MOM

I know

ZUZU

…

ZUZU'S MOM

You forgot about the plié, huh?

ZUZU

I don't know

ZUZU'S MOM

During the bridge, you forgot to do the little plié. That's why you stumbled in the transition.

ZUZU
I don't remember

ZUZU'S MOM
Other than that it was a really, really good audition.

MAEVE and LUKE walk past ZUZU and her mom on their way out of the dressing room.

MAEVE
Oh hey Zuzu

LUKE
Oh hey Zuzu

MAEVE
Good job

LUKE
Really really good job, Zuzu

He smiles at her.

LUKE
You were really great

5

ZUZU alone.

ZUZU
People say I dance with a lot of *grace* and that I'm beautiful
and above-average and stuff.
Here's what they don't say.
They don't say I'm sensational.
They don't say I take their breath away.
They don't say they could watch me forever.
They don't say they cry when they watch me dance.
When they watch Amina dance, they cry.
I know. Because I cry when I watch Amina dance.

My Mom asked me to dance for her cancer. She saw a
documentary about this woman who did a dance and it cured
her cancer and so she asked me if I would do a dance for her
and my Mom is not normally like that but she was feeling
really emotional at the time and she kept breaking down all
the time so I did this solo at the year end recital for my Mom
and her cancer. And I tried to make it the best dance I had
ever done. I tried to like *feel things* with my arms and my legs.
I tried to make people feel things with my arms and my legs.
But it was just an ordinary dance, really. A lot of people didn't
know it was about my Mom's cancer at all. They thought it
was about whatever our dances are usually about. Flowers.
Or sailors, you know. Not cancer. I didn't make them cry.
I didn't make myself cry. I don't even think I made my Mom
cry. She told me that she liked it. But she didn't cry. And it
didn't cure her cancer, so. Her cancer actually got worse after
that, so. It was just an ordinary dance.

Luke says I'm a genius dancer but he's lying to me because
he's in love with me. Luke has dandruff. I know because I was
playing with his hair the other day and at the base of his hair
near his scalp were all these flakes of scalp sitting in his hair
like dead ants that had just crawled out of a hole and died.

Petals fall from the sky like flakes of dandruff as ZUZU dances the audition piece for Gandhi. She's not that great. CONNIE appears and dances the part of Gandhi with her.

The stars come out.

LUKE and his MOM driving home from dance.

LUKE'S MOM
You sleepy?

LUKE
…

LUKE'S MOM
You look sleepy

LUKE
Yeah

LUKE'S MOM
It takes it out of you, doesn't it?

LUKE
Yeah

LUKE'S MOM
…

LUKE
…

LUKE'S MOM
…

LUKE
…

LUKE'S MOM
…

LUKE

How was your day?

LUKE'S MOM

Oh you know

LUKE

…

…

…

LUKE'S MOM

I think that new priest candidate is coming

From California

So that's good

LUKE

…

LUKE'S MOM

Apparently it's some kind of secret

She's not telling her congregation that she's thinking of leaving, so

We have to be all secretive about it

…

…

She's flying cross-country on a *Tuesday* so she won't be missed, so

I don't know

It sounds kind of crazy to me but

Who knows

She's our only candidate, so

Hopefully she's not too crazy

LUKE

She's flying cross-country?

LUKE'S MOM

Yeah

LUKE
And she's not telling anybody?

LUKE'S MOM
Apparently

LUKE
That's cool

LUKE'S MOM
It's stressful… It's more stressful than it's cool

…

…

…

…

…

I just hope this lady from California does more than give good sermons. Good sermons don't bring in crowds. We need someone who's a go-getter. She's fifty-two, so. I don't know. I was hoping for someone younger.

LUKE
Yeah

…

…

…

…

                    LUKE
All I want
Is someone to drive me
Driving in cars………………
Driving in cars at night…
Driving in cars at night with the rain
spraying the dashboard and a seat warmer
that makes my butt hot. Hot like when I used
to sit my naked ass on the radiator at home
growing up. A hot butt makes me sleepy. And

I'd get so sleepy. Riding in cars at night. But it's the delicious kind of sleepy. Where you wish you could stay in that liminal state forever watching the raindrops on the windshield and the world blurring by.........and my Mom...listening to my Mom... remembering listening to my Mom.... all I want is to be in a car at night, sleepy and listening to my Mom

…

…

……

LUKE'S MOM
How's dance?

LUKE
Huh?

LUKE'S MOM
How was dance? Did you learn something?

LUKE
It was fine

LUKE'S MOM
What are you working on now? Are you still doing that sailor–

LUKE
No we switched. We're doing Citizens

…

…

…

We're doing this whole thing with Gandhi

LUKE'S MOM
That sounds fun

…

…

And you're liking it?

He shrugs.

LUKE'S MOM
Because you don't have to keep doing it if you're not liking it.
You could do ice skating / or music

LUKE
No I like it!

LUKE'S MOM
Just as long as you're liking it

LUKE
I like it

LUKE'S MOM
Okay
…
…
…
That's good
…
…

LUKE	LUKE'S MOM
…	…
…	…
…	…
…	…
…	…

Somewhere, moon, window etc.

CONNIE
Dear God
Please
Please

Please give me
the part of
Gandhi
I promise I'll do
a good job,
please Lord
Please let it be
me, just this one
time, please, just
this once,
let it
be
me
…
…
..
.

6

THE GIRLS and LUKE are lined up in leotards and spandex – ready for class. A little army.

ALL THE GIRLS
If I could change the world through dance
If I could change the world by dancing with my body
If I could dance away my mom's cancer
And my friend Alyssa's depression
And the way she won't stop eating skittles when she's hungry
Instead of eating proper food
If I could dance away world hunger
And all violence against women
And all pets without a home
And all the sadness
Allll the sadness
All the sadness and the meanness
If I could dance and nobody would ever want to kill another person again
Or be racist again
Or feel alone at night again
Or abandon their pets without a home again
That's what I would do
That's what I would do
That's what I want to do with my LIFE

DANCE TEACHER PAT
Alright girls
Great auditions
It wasn't easy but I've made my decision

They all hold hands – nervous, expectant.

ALL THE GIRLS
I want to dance
I want to dance
I want to heal the world through DANCE

I want to dance
I want to dance
I want to feel alive through DANCE
I want to dance
I want to dance
I want to dance

DANCE TEACHER PAT
And the role of Gandhi will be played by…

ALL THE GIRLS
I want to dance
I want to dance
I want to dance
I want to dance
I want to dance
I want to dance

DANCE TEACHER PAT
Connie!

> *ALL THE GIRLS gasp and grunt. They gather supportively around CONNIE who is beaming.*

DANCE TEACHER PAT
But there's a twist…

> *THE GIRLS freeze – terrified.*

DANCE TEACHER PAT
In addition to the role of Gandhi, I have created another role. The role of *the spirit of Gandhi.*

> *(Oh my god! Another chance at a featured part!)*

DANCE TEACHER PAT
And the role of *the spirit of Gandhi* will be played by …………
……………………………………………………………………………
……………………………………………………………………………
………………………………………………………**ZUZU!**

THE GIRLS scream bloodcurdling screams. They gather around ZUZU supportively, who is on the verge of tears. LUKE throws his arms around her. All genuine.

MAEVE
Congratulations!

LUKE
Congratulations!

AMINA
Congratulations, Zuzu, you're gonna be great!

ASHLEE
That's so exciting

ZUZU
Thanks guys

DANCE TEACHER PAT *(To ZUZU.)*
Are you happy?

ZUZU *(Barely able to speak.)*
Yes

DANCE TEACHER PAT
It's a big responsibility, Zuzu. Think of all the people the spirit of Gandhi has inspired. Martin Luther King… John Lennon… That's *you*. You have to show us that.

She nods.

DANCE TEACHER PAT
Alright, Citizens spread apart. Connie, sit on the floor.

He points to the floor.

DANCE TEACHER PAT teaches THE GIRLS the chorus part. CONNIE sits on the floor as "Gandhi."

DANCE TEACHER PAT
We're going to start with a nice sternum expansion…

He demonstrates – his arms extended, his chest open…

THE GIRLS copy him.

DANCE TEACHER PAT
Let your heart go out – out – out – - – - – - - - – - – - - – - – - -

7

Later. SOFIA and AMINA are huddled outside the dance studio in their tracksuits with their dance bags hung over their shoulders.

SOFIA
It's not that big of a deal. The Gandhi dance is lame anyway

AMINA
Yeah

SOFIA
Gandhi doesn't even do anything. Connie just sits on the floor

AMINA
But the *spirit* of Gandhi…

SOFIA
Whatever. Zuzu's going to mess it up

AMINA
…

SOFIA
You know she's going to mess it up. Dance Teacher Pat's just trying to be nice. He can't give you the solo *every time*

AMINA
You don't think he's mad at me?

SOFIA
Nah. The dance is lame so he gave it to Zuzu

AMINA
You think so?

SOFIA
Oh yeah. I know so

ZUZU in the other room working on the Spirit of Gandhi solo with DANCE TEACHER PAT. We hear him as we've never heard him before – mean, vicious, punishing...

DANCE TEACHER PAT *(Offstage.)*
Are you an idiot?

ZUZU *(Offstage.)*
I don't know

DANCE TEACHER PAT
Then why are you acting like one?

ZUZU
I don't know

DANCE TEACHER PAT
You don't know?

ZUZU
I don't know what you're asking me!

DANCE TEACHER PAT
I'm asking you to do it again. And do it right this time.
...
And don't try so hard. It's embarrassing.

SOFIA and AMINA listening to ZUZU and DANCE TEACHER PAT in the other room...

SOFIA *(Hushed.)*
<Should we wait for her?>

AMINA *(Hushed.)*
<I don't know>

DANCE TEACHER PAT
No. Again

SOFIA *(Calling out.)*
Bye, Zu...

AMINA *(Calling out.)*
Bye, Zu...

They listen, a little terrified...

DANCE TEACHER PAT
Again

SOFIA *(Not unkind.)*
Bet you fifty dollars she has a nervous breakdown by the end
of the week

AMINA (*To SOFIA.*)
Zuzu's a good dancer

SOFIA
I know

AMINA
She's really talented

SOFIA
She is!

ZUZU left alone in the studio, working with DANCE TEACHER PAT.

8

The next day. ZUZU's MOM has come to the studio to speak with DANCE TEACHER PAT. ZUZU is sitting on the toilet in her tights and leotard, mortified.

THE GIRLS are at the barre, warming up.

AMINA
Alright so assume first position and then we're just going to go through the pliés

Classical music plays…

AMINA
Demi plié and…

…

…

Demi plié and…

…	**ZUZU'S MOM**
…	Zuzu is not allowed to be the best
…	dancer she can be. You don't let her
Grand plié…	
…	**DANCE TEACHER PAT**
…	I don't let her?
…	
…	**ZUZU'S MOTHER**
…	You purposely intimidate her!
…	
…	**DANCE TEACHER PAT**
…	That's my job!
…	
…	**ZUZU'S MOTHER**
…	You put her down. You make her think
…	she can't do it!
…	

	DANCE TEACHER PAT
...	I teach! I correct! It's up to her whether
...	or not she thinks she can do it!
...	
...	**ZUZU'S MOM**
...	Listen to me.............
...	There's no such thing as talent
...	People plant it in their minds
...	Whether they're good at this
...	Or bad at that
...	And they become whatever *you tell them they are*
...	
...	**DANCE TEACHER PAT**
...	Do you honestly believe that?
...	
...	**ZUZU'S MOM**
...	I'm just saying that geniuses have had
...	their cocks sucked by / a lot of people
...	
THE GIRLS ears	**DANCE TEACHER PAT**
perk up. What is	Okay, please don't talk like that
going on ???!	
...	**ZUZU'S MOM** *(Hushed.)*
...	*You are destroying my child*
AMINA	
Fourth position	**DANCE TEACHER PAT**
...	What do you want me to do?
Demi plié and...	
...	**ZUZU'S MOM**
...	I want you to tell her that she's special
Demi plié and...	I want you to tell her that she's a genius
...	
...	**DANCE TEACHER PAT**
...	I can't / do that
...	

47

...	**ZUZU'S MOM**
...	I want you to whisper in her ear
...	that she's *amazing* and that she takes your
...	breath away *every. single. time.* she dances.
...	*That's!* What I want you to do
...	
...	**DANCE TEACHER PAT**
...	If I don't see it / I can't
...	
...	**ZUZU'S MOM**
...	She's only a child
...	
...	**DANCE TEACHER PAT**
...	Yes, well
...	Children live *in the world*
...	And it's not some special world
...	Where everyone gets a chance
...	There is such a thing as talent
...	And we all know it when we see it
...	And there's such a thing as charisma
(They stop dancing.)	And momentum
...	And destiny
...	And we know it when we feel it, so
...	Don't tell me
...	To go against the world
...	
...	**ZUZU'S MOM**
...	You make her! You make her! I'm saying
...	that you make her!
...	...
...	...
...	So make her!
..	...
.	I'm asking you to make her
.	
.	

48

AMINA

Other side

…

Demi plié aaannnnddd….

…

…

Demi plié aaannnnddd….

….

Grand plié…….

…

…

…

Bend…….

…

And come up……

…

…

Second position

…

…

Demi plié and….

…

…

Demi plié and………

…

…

Grand plié….

…

…

…

ASHLEE *(Whispering.)*
Pussy

AMINA
Bend at the waist…

…

…

…

ASHLEE *(Whispering.)*
Pussy

SOFIA *(Whispering.)*
Pussy

AMINA
And…come…up…
Fourth position
Demi plié

CONNIE *(Whispering.)*
Pussy

ASHLEE *(Whispering.)*
Pussy

MAEVE/SOFIA *(Whispering.)*
Pussy

CONNIE *(Whispering.)*
Pussy

ASHLEE *(Whispering.)*
Pussy

LUKE *(Whispering.)*
Pussy

AMINA
Bend and…

…

…

Come…up…

ASHLEE/CONNIE/MAEVE/SOFIA/LUKE *(Whispering.)*

…

…

Pusssyyyyy

AMINA *(Devilish, but with a normal speaking voice.)*
And move your pussy into fifth position

(Victory!!!!!!!!!)

AMINA
Demi plié and…

…

Demi plié and…

…

Grand plié

…

…

Bend at the pussy…and…bring your pussy back up….

DANCE TEACHER PAT comes back into the room.

DANCE TEACHER PAT
How's it going, girls?

AMINA
Good. We're almost done with warm up

DANCE TEACHER PAT
Where's Zuzu?

Blank stares.

> *(ZUZU still alone on the
> toilet. Somehow, some way
> she's grown little sharp teeth.
> Like fangs. She bites her
> forearm hard. Harder. Blood
> spurts out. She chews off
> a chunk of her arm.)*

DANCE TEACHER PAT
ZUUUZUUUUUUUUUUUUUUU

> **ZUZU**
> YESSSS???
>
> *(She jumps up off the toilet
> and dashes out of the bathroom
> into the studio, her arm still
> pulsing blood.)*

ZUZU *(Still with her fangs.)*
I'm here

DANCE TEACHER PAT
We're going to run through the number
Everybody ready?

> *They nod.*

LUKE *(To ZUZU.)*
You okay?

ZUZU
I'm fine

DANCE TEACHER PAT

5-6-7-8!

> *They dance.*

> *Except it's not really like Gandhi.*

> *It's more like baby sexy robots. Bloodsucking robots who want to
> destroy the world and then fuck it after it's dead.*

> *They are barely wearing any clothes. They are touching their bodies.
> They are gnashing their teeth – all of them have fangs now. Sharp,
> pointy teeth.*

> *Music plays. Think "Buttons" by The Pussycat Dolls.*

They are climbing up the walls. MAEVE is chewing on the light bulbs –
glass in her mouth. Glass is crushed beneath their feet. ZUZU does her
special part. She's awesome.

DANCE TEACHER PAT
Alright girls. I don't know what **THE FUCK** this is. But it's not
Gandhi.

Zzzzzz. The lights go out with an electric hiss except for one bright light
shining down from Heaven on…… ASHLEE…panting, still baby sex robot
power, etc. Half-dressed, her hair sticking to her forehead.

The buzz of the music beneath her. She talks to us. Not vain, not bragging.
Just genuinely pondering the possibility…

ASHLEE
I think I might be frickin' gorgeous
My ass, especially
Might be frickin' gorgeous
I wish I could show you my ass but I'm only thirteen
My ass has been described as "epic"
An "Epic Bottom"
Someone said that to me once. He said: "You have an Epic Bottom"
It sounds a little creepy now, but it didn't sound creepy when he said it
Men like to stroke my ass when they see it
They pull me over their laps
And they stroke my ass
Like it were a talisman
Or a worry stone
Worn perfectly smooth and round
By time
Except it's the opposite of time
I'm young
I just got popped out like this
Me and my perfect ass
Like two little deer droppings
Smooshed together

Frickin' epic
Also I have a pretty face
I have a really nice face, I think
I really like my face
And I have great tits, so
I feel really lucky
I feel really *blessed* or whatever
Let's just admit it
I'm a frickin' catch
I walk down the street and I feel everybody looking at me, you know
I'm not trying to brag
I'm serious. I promise. I'm not
I'm just trying to figure this out
I'm just trying to be real for a moment
I think it's important to be real about things like this
Like sometimes people post pictures online
And all of their friends are like
Whoa. Gorgeous
Look at you girl. You could be a model. KaBOOM!!!!!
Why do people lie to people like that?
I'm serious
I don't get it
Just say: That's a great picture of you! Nice shot! You look great!
Not: "You're gorgeous"
Not: "KaBOOM"
It's like what exploded? Nothing exploded. I don't see anything explosive about that picture. Why are you pretending that something exploded?
I don't get it
Just tell the truth

She's off-track, she catches herself, she starts again…

ASHLEE
Here's the other thing
I'm really frickin' smart
I am. I'm smarter than most people I meet
I'm probably smarter than you
And not just liberal arts bullshit
I'm good at math
People are always like lollllllll
I'm bad at math wahhh
Like that makes them cool
No it doesn't
You suck at math
That doesn't make you cool
Math makes you cool
It's not that hard to be good at math
Math is actually the easiest section of the SAT to get a perfect
score on, so
If you just study
It's the most "study-able" section
So I guess you didn't study
That doesn't make you cool
That just makes you lazy and shortsighted about your future
Seriously people, it's not that hard to be good at math if you
frickin try
Are you even trying people???
"Wahhhh I'm bad at math"
Shut the fuck up and stop whining and just think about the
problem for a minute
It's not that hard
It's not like you have to write a fucking poem
There are like *rules*
There's like *an answer*
I don't even have parents who can help me and I *still* ace it
Because I'm not a moron

She collects herself. A little nervous from saying all this out loud.

55

ASHLEE

Anyway. So I never say this stuff to anybody because I'm afraid they're going to hate me. But I think about it sometimes. And sometimes it makes me feel ashamed. Like I'm a bad person. And I want to bury it down deep. Never acknowledge it. Keep my eyes on the pavement when I feel men looking at me and just pretend I don't exist.

…

Like every time someone has ever told me that I'm beautiful I say: "No."

…

This guy, he said to me, "You're really beautiful" and I just said: "No." It's like a reflex

…

You're beautiful. *No.* You're smart. *No.* You're funny. *No.* You're beautiful.

She shakes her head, no.

ASHLEE

But sometimes I wonder what would happen, if I really went for it

…

I mean, I'm a little afraid of what would happen if I really went for it

…

…

Over the course of the following, ASHLEE grows taller. Her shadow become twelve-feet long. Her eyes turn red. Her fangs lengthen. Her voice becomes the voice of some vengeful, ancient pagan god. THE GIRLS stare at her in awe. The baby sexy robot music still humming…

ASHLEE

Like if I tried. If I really, really tried. Like if I acknowledged it.
Just embraced it. Like if I walked down the street and looked
those men straight in the eyes and said: "Yes, I'm beautiful and
I'm gonna get a perfect score on the SAT, Math, Reading *and*
Writing, motherfucker, and yes I'm only thirteen years old
now but just wait ten more years because one day I'm going
to be a FUCKING SURGEON, one day I'm going be
a FUCKING GENIUS POET *and* running my own
company, one day I'm going to be even more ridiculously
attractive than I am now *and* GREAT AT SEX and
I'm going to cut people open like it's my fucking job because
it *is* my fucking job and I'm going to make you my
bitch, you motherfucking cunt-munching piece of shit prick
I *am* your god. I *am* your second coming. I *am* your
mother and I'm smarter than you and more attractive
than you and better than you at everything that you
love and you're going to get down on your knees and
worship my mind, my mind *and my body* and I'm gonnna
be the motherfucking KING of your motherfucking
world, I'm going to be the KING OF EVERYBODY'S
MOTHERFUCKING WORLD, and you're going cum
just by eating my cunt, the taste of my cum is going
to make you cum because it'll be the greatest sexual
pleasure you have ever known *just tasting me* and
the words I say are going to be the greatest fucking words
that you've ever heard and the things I do are going
to be the greatest fucking things you've ever witnessed.
That's what I've got inside this tiny fucking body
of mine and I don't have to deny it I don't have
to disown it I don't have to be ashamed of it
I can shout it from the rooftops because you are
all my motherfucking BITCH

She shrinks.

The lights snap back to fluorescents. The light of Heaven is gone.

ASHLEE stands alone, a little scared. A little exhausted. A little perplexed.

ASHLEE *(A genuine question, she asks us…)*
What am I going to do with all this power?

…

What am I going to do with all this power?

…

Huh?

…

…

I don't know.

…

…

…

…

…

…

…

…

…

…

…

I hope I don't pussy out.

MAEVE howls like a wolf.

THE GIRLS gnash their fangs and strike a final pose – ZUZU, fabulous as the "Spirit of Gandhi" and in the middle of the pack.

9

AMINA catches ZUZU after the run-through.

AMINA
Hey Zu

ZUZU
Yeah?

AMINA
You looked really good out there

ZUZU
Oh. Thanks

AMINA
You totally killed that solo

ZUZU
Really?

AMINA
Yeah your turns were really good. They were really centered

ZUZU
Yeah they felt good. I felt on top of myself

AMINA
You were really, really on top of yourself. And you looked clean

ZUZU
Okay good. I was worried

AMINA
Don't be worried. You're doing awesome

ZUZU
Thanks I need to work on my side aerial but–

AMINA
You'll get it

ZUZU
Yeah

AMINA
It took me like two years to get my side aerial

ZUZU
Yeah

AMINA
You'll definitely get it

ZUZU
I hope so

AMINA
For sure

> *They smile at each other.*

ZUZU
Hey. You wanna come over? My mom's making pizza

AMINA
Oh … I don't think I can

ZUZU
Oh

AMINA
I just– I wanna get to bed early

ZUZU
Okay

AMINA
Sorry. I just–
I hate not sleeping before competitions

ZUZU
No, I get it. I hate not sleeping, too

They smile at each other.

ZUZU
Have you thought about what you're doing for the summer?

AMINA
Oh!

ZUZU
I was thinking about maybe applying for the ballet fellowship
at Pittsburgh Ballet?

AMINA
That'd be cool

ZUZU
Yeah I don't know if I'll get in. But it'd be so cool

…

…

I need to focus on my ballet

AMINA
Yeah Dance Teacher Pat wants to send me to Russia

ZUZU
To Russia?

AMINA
Yeah, he wants me to go and train with this ballet company
in Russia. I don't know. It sounds kinda intense

ZUZU
Intense is good, though

AMINA
I'm kinda scared

ZUZU
That's how you get better

AMINA

…

…

Yeah I think Sabina went

ZUZU

Oh?

AMINA

Yeah like when she was in high school

ZUZU

Cool.

…

…

AMINA

Pittsburgh Ballet is supposed to be really good, though.

ZUZU

Yeah I don't know

AMINA

I know this girl Eliza who went, and she really loved it.
She made a lot of really great friends

…

Maybe you could also apply for the Philly program? That's
supposed to be good, too.

ZUZU

It's expensive, though

AMINA

I bet there are like scholarships and things

ZUZU

Yeah I should probably look into that

AMINA

…

ZUZU

…

AMINA

…

ZUZU
Is Russia expensive?

AMINA
I don't know. I'm not paying

They smile at each other.

AMINA
I think Pittsburgh will be awesome

ZUZU
Hey Amina?

AMINA
Yeah

ZUZU
Don't be mad at me
But I think I need to stop talking to you about dance for awhile
Like I still love you a lot
You're still my best friend
But I just might not be able to talk to you about some things

AMINA

…

ZUZU
And I may have to close my eyes, sometimes, when you dance
But it's not because I don't love you
It's just because I might need to take a break from watching you
And from talking to you
For awhile

…

…

…

Sorry

AMINA
Uh

ZUZU
Is that mean?

AMINA
Uh. No I don't think so

ZUZU
I still really really really love you

AMINA
I know
I just–

ZUZU
…

AMINA
I don't know
…
I don't know what to say

ZUZU
…

AMINA
That's fine

ZUZU
Yeah?

AMINA
I totally get it

ZUZU
You do?

AMINA
Yeah

ZUZU
Thanks

AMINA
…

ZUZU
…

AMINA
…

ZUZU
…

AMINA
What kind of pizza are you having?

ZUZU
I don't know
…
Canadian bacon and olives. That's what my mom likes

AMINA
Cool

ZUZU
…

AMINA
…

ZUZU
…

AMINA

Sorry

ZUZU

What?

AMINA

I just don't really have anything to say

DANCE TEACHER PAT appears. He's locking up.

DANCE TEACHER PAT

Hey girls

ZUZU/AMINA

Hiii

DANCE TEACHER PAT

You're still here?

ZUZU

I'm going home. Goodnight, Amina

AMINA

Goodnight

ZUZU bolts.

AMINA stands there watching DANCE TEACHER PAT lock up.

AMINA

Are you mad at me?

He looks at her.

DANCE TEACHER PAT

I'm not mad at you

AMINA

…

DANCE TEACHER PAT *(Crouching down to her height to look her straight in the eye.)* But Amina

AMINA
Yes?

DANCE TEACHER PAT
Next time you audition for me I want you to remember that
I can tell how much you want it

AMINA
…

DANCE TEACHER PAT
Understood?

She nods.

DANCE TEACHER PAT
Don't get lazy

He sort of swats her butt. It's not sexual???????? But also weird and uncomfortable for a a grown-ass man to be swatting a thirteen-year-old's butt. AMINA is horrified. And also, she loves it.

AMINA
I won't

She scampers off.

DANCE TEACHER PAT *(Calling after her.)*
SHOW ME YOU WANT IT

AMINA scampering, from a distance…

DANCE TEACHER PAT *(Half-hearted down the hallway.)*
I WANNA SEE THAT YOU WANT IT….

She's gone.

DANCE TEACHER PAT alone in his studio. It's late. He should pack up his things and head out for the night. But he doesn't feel like moving.

He sighs a world-weary sigh.

DANCE TEACHER PAT
I guess I should go home

10

Philadelphia. The day of the competition.

ALL THE GIRLS in a different dressing room getting ready. They curl their hair, paint their faces elaborate colors, apply fake eyelashes. CONNIE is dressed like Gandhi. ZUZU is in a brilliant gold Spirit of Gandhi costume distinct from the Citizens.

ALL THE GIRLS still have their fangs.

SOFIA
If I have a child he is *not* getting circumcised

AMINA
Really?

SOFIA
Yeah

AMINA
Why?

SOFIA
Because it's barbaric to cut-off a piece of your baby's penis

CONNIE
My dad is circumcised

SOFIA
I'm not judging. Just not my kid.

ASHLEE sneezes.

CONNIE	**ASHLEE**
Luke are you circumcised?	*<sorry!>*

LUKE
Um

ASHLEE sneezes.

AMINA	ASHLEE
Everyone is circumcised	*<sorry!>*

SOFIA
Everyone is not circumcised!

MAEVE
My kid's going to be circumcised because my mom is Jewish so I sorta have to

CONNIE
I'm not Jewish and my kid's going to be circumcised too

MAEVE
What about you Luke?

LUKE
Um

ASHLEE
The thing is – you have to think about the locker room. Because my dad says that boys who are uncircumcised get made fun of a lot in the locker room. And that's really not something you want to do to your thirteen-year-old kid, you know

SOFIA
Yeah but sex is better with an uncircumcised penis

ALL THE GIRLS
…

SOFIA
It's true

MAEVE
How do you know that?

SOFIA
Everybody knows it. It's like a fact.

CONNIE
I bet you're circumcised, Luke, aren't you?

SOFIA
It's like I will never, ever, ever, ever, ever marry a man who's going to make me circumcise my kid. That's just a deal breaker, you know?

MAEVE
Maybe Amina was circumcised when she was a baby and nobody told her and *that's* why she can't masturbate

CONNIE
What are you talking / about?

ASHLEE
No!

CONNIE
Maeve!

| **ASHLEE** | **CONNIE** |
| That's just wrong! | You're crazy |

AMINA *(Despondent.)*
Do you think there's something wrong with me?

SOFIA
Nah, you're probably just slow

ASHLEE
Yeah you're probably just developmentally delayed or something. Don't worry about it

SOFIA
Yeah, you're probably just a late bloomer, Amina

ASHLEE
Yeah. Everyone's on a different time frame

ZUZU
Hey Luke? Can you sew this into my head?

LUKE
Sure

LUKE sews a flower into ZUZU's hair.

SOFIA
I bet you're not going to have any sex until you're like thirty-five and then one day you'll just explode with all these sexual feelings and you'll be like way more sexual than the rest of us and we'll all be married and you'll be like a sexy, older woman with all these lovers

CONNIE
Totally. That's totally you, Amina

AMINA *(Even more despondent.)*
But I don't want to wait until I'm thirty-five

MAEVE
Maybe it's already happened
Maybe it just feels different for you
And you've already felt it
And you didn't even know

LUKE
Connie, did you bring your lucky horse?

CONNIE
Yeah, it's over there

There's a beautiful Appaloosa amidst the carnage of the table.

SOFIA hands it to LUKE.

LUKE
Okay, *phew!*

AMINA
I need to touch it, too

ASHLEE
What about you, Zu? When do you think you'll have sex?

ZUZU
I don't care

ASHLEE
What do you mean you don't care?!

ZUZU
As long as I can dance, then I don't care

SOFIA
She's lying

ZUZU
I've wanted to be a dancer since I was two years old. That's all I want

SOFIA
Two year olds don't even have wants

ZUZU
Yes they do
I was two
And I wanted to be a dancer
The best dancer
In the entire world
I wanted to be a professional dancer when I was two

CONNIE
Me too

MAEVE
I don't know what I wanted when I was two
I think I just wanted
You know

Water

And stuff like that

Their faces are painted now – bright, freakish colors. They look like monster aliens with their little fangs.

CONNIE *(Applying her eyelashes.)*
I remember this dude from Germany who used to visit my parents
I don't even remember why he was there…
He was my parents' friend?
He was German?
He was only in town for a short while
This was like three years ago
I don't know
He would come and he would put his belly against my back
and he would put his hand on my shoulder and he would sing
along when I played the piano
Like is that normal?
I got very nervous that it wasn't okay
But no one said anything about it
My parents saw him do it and everything
So I guess it was okay?

ASHLEE
Did you see his penis?

CONNIE
No!

ASHLEE
Then it's fine

AMINA
I don't know, I find it all very confusing

SOFIA
What's confusing?

AMINA
I don't know

MAEVE
I saw this penis once

ASHLEE
What?

SOFIA
Was it romantic?

MAEVE
No

CONNIE
Was it your brother's penis?

MAEVE
Never mind

SOFIA
Was it your dad's penis?

MAEVE
I SAID NEVER MIND!

DANCE TEACHER PAT *(Entering.)*
Hey girls how's it going

ALL THE GIRLS
Good, Hi Dance Teacher Pat!, etc.

DANCE TEACHER PAT
Are you ready to go?

ALL THE GIRLS
Yeah we're ready, etc. pretty much!

DANCE TEACHER PAT
Let me see what you look like

 They line up in their costumes, face paint, etc. They look good.

DANCE TEACHER PAT
You look good. Alright. Circle up

 They do.

DANCE TEACHER PAT

Now I know there's a lot of pressure on you
But I want to take a minute
And I want you to close your eyes

They do.

DANCE TEACHER PAT

And I want you to forget about all the steps…
Everything we've worked on…
I want you to forget about being in Philadelphia, away from
your families…
And Nationals and going to Tampa Bay…
It doesn't exist
…
…
Just breathe in

They do.

DANCE TEACHER PAT

And let it all go

They exhale.

DANCE TEACHER PAT

Now I want you to take a moment
And I want you to think about *alllll* the people in the world
People who are struggling
People who aren't as fortunate as you
People who don't have parents like you do
Who pay for them to go to dance class
Who buy things for them
I want you to think about children
Who don't get to go to school
They have to go to *work*

MAEVE suppresses a giggle.

DANCE TEACHER PAT
I'll wait

MAEVE
Sorry! I just get nervous when <*I have to close my eyes...*>

He glares at her.

DANCE TEACHER PAT *(To MAEVE.)*
You ready?

MAEVE nods.

DANCE TEACHER PAT
I want you to think about children
Who don't have anyone to turn to
Who don't have anyone they can trust
Or they can talk to
Who are being abused
Who are living in garbage, sometimes, *literal garbage*
Their beds, their houses
And no one touches them, no one loves them, no one
wonders when they're coming home at night or asks them
how their day was

THE GIRLS are somber now. Maybe SOFIA is crying a little.

*AMINA and CONNIE have their eyes cracked open, a little skeptical.
They catch each other's eyes and smile.*

DANCE TEACHER PAT
You girls don't realize how lucky you are
You don't realize that the problems you struggle with
Are not real problems
That the world is full of suffering
And you're tasting only a tiny part of it

   ...

   ,,,

   ...

...   (it shifts, slightly... becomes very small, quiet, internal...
...   like a tiny, private vigil...
...   the audience should register what he's saying
...   as something that's really happening in the world, right now,
...   as he speaks...)
...
...

You breathe in............................. Someone dies......

He snaps his fingers, quietly.

DANCE TEACHER PAT
Another person just died

snaps

DANCE TEACHER PAT
Another person just died

snaps

DANCE TEACHER PAT
Another person just died

snaps

DANCE TEACHER PAT
Another person is on their knees...
In their closet...
Crying, in so much pain...
Right *now*, right in this instant

ALL THE GIRLS
...

DANCE TEACHER PAT
I want you to think about all the people in the world who are
suffering...

...
...

And I want you to go out there

…

…

And I want you to *dance for them*

> *They open their eyes. They all smile at each other – full of purpose,*
> *very powerful.*

DANCE TEACHER PAT
You ready?

> *They are.*

DANCE TEACHER PAT
Knock 'em dead

ALL THE GIRLS *(This is their studio chant; they bark it.)*
HARRINGTON DANCE WORKS
EAT
SLEEP
DANCE
EAT
SLEEP
DANCE
EAT
SLEEP
WIN!

> *THE GIRLS and LUKE run out the door in an impassioned flurry.*

> *DANCE TEACHER PAT calls after ZUZU.*

DANCE TEACHER PAT
Hey Zuzu

ZUZU *(Mumbling, dying.)*
Yeah???

DANCE TEACHER PAT
Come here for a second

She does.

DANCE TEACHER PAT
I took a big chance on you, you know that, right?

She nods.

DANCE TEACHER PAT
Prove me right. Okay?

He puts a hand on her shoulder. It's intimate. Almost kind.

DANCE TEACHER PAT
I like to be right

(It's almost a joke.)

DANCE TEACHER PAT
Philly. Akron. Lanoka. It all starts here.

He points to her heart.

DANCE TEACHER PAT
The moment you decide to win is the moment you win. A new chapter for Zuzu.

She nods.

DANCE TEACHER PAT
You can do it

ZUZU blinks and then bolts to catch up with the other kids.

11

Backstage. THE GIRLS are nervous – shaking out their feet and hands.

AMINA holds ZUZU by the neck, nose-to-nose. She coaches her.

AMINA
Just focus on your breath
Your breath and your feet
And remember to use your face

ZUZU
I know

AMINA
I know that you know. I'm just reminding you

SOFIA
Guys

AMINA *(To ZUZU.)*
You've totally got this

ASHLEE *(To CONNIE.)*
Are you nervous?

CONNIE
No

ASHLEE
You're gonna be great!

SOFIA
Guys

CONNIE
All I do is sit on a the floor

AMINA
Come on guys, let's pray. *(Indicating.)* Connie.

They circle up and pray. CONNIE leads them.

CONNIE
Dear God
Please help us to do our best
And please help us to win

SOFIA
Guys

AMINA
Shhh!

CONNIE
It's been a hard week
And we've been working really hard–

SOFIA
guysss

LUKE
Shhh!

CONNIE
And we deserve this
So please anoint each girl and bring us to victory.

ASHLEE
Amen!

EVERYBODY
AMEN!

SOFIA
Guys. I think there's something wrong

SOFIA pulls down her tights. There's blood everywhere.

SOFIA
Oh no, oh no

ASHLEE
You're fine! You're fine!

MAN ON THE MIC
Girls, you're on deck! This is your two-minute warning

CONNIE
Oh my god, / we're doing it

ZUZU
I'm going to throw up

SOFIA
I can't go out there!

ASHLEE
Sofia! Look at me! It's two minutes and thirty seconds. You're going to be fine

LUKE
Where's Maeve?

CONNIE *(Shaking out her hands, in the zone, under her breath.)*
Fuzz, fuzz, fuzz, fu-fuzz, fuzz, fuzz

LUKE
Guys?! Where's Maeve???????

AMINA *(Calling.)*
Maeve!

MAEVE comes sprinting around the corner.

AMINA
It's two minutes, Maeve!! Get in line!

MAEVE
You guys, you guys! I just got wind of our competition

ZUZU
And?

MAEVE
They have boys

AMINA
We have boys

MAEVE
We have Luke
But they have like *advanced-level* boys
They have boys that do turns

> *THE GIRLS gasp.*

LUKE
(I do turns sometimes)

MAEVE
And flips

> *THE GIRLS gasp.*

MAEVE
They have like: *dancing boys*
Boys who can do fouettes
BOYS DRESSED UP AS NEWSIES
WHO ARE DOING LIFTS
WITH OTHER GIRLS!!!
THEY ARE LIFTING THEM OVER THEIR HEADS
AND SELLING THEIR NEWSPAPERS
AND SPINNING SO FAST
AS FAST AS AMINA

SOFIA
No!

MAEVE
YES!

SOFIA
<Fuck!>

ZUZU
We're going to be eliminated / in the first round!!!!

SOFIA
This is so humiliating

AMINA
What are we going to do???????

ASHLEE *(Quietly.)*
…
…
…
We're going to destroy them

CONNIE
But the judges are partial to–

ASHLEE
We have to destroy them

CONNIE
But dancing boys are–

AMINA
She's right. Dancing boys are unbeatable.

ASHLEE *(In a huddle, whispered, mean…)*
WE'RE FUCKING MONSTERS, BABIES, AND WE'RE
GONNA MAKE THEM EAT THEIR DICKS AND DIE

ALL THE GIRLS
…

ASHLEE
WE'RE GONNA BLEED 'EM FROM THEIR STOMACHS
AND MAKE THEM LICK *THE BLOOD FROM THE STAGE*

CONNIE
Um, Ashlee. I / don't–

SOFIA
WE'RE GONNA MAKE THEM FINGER US UNTIL
THEIR FINGERS FALL OFF AND THEN WE'RE GONNA
EAT THEIR FINGERS IN FRONT OF THEIR FACES!!!!!!

ASHLEE
YESSSSSSSSSSSSSSSSSssssssssss

MAEVE
WE'RE GONNA GET PREGNANT WITH THEIR BABIES
AND THEN WE'RE GONNA RIP THOSE BABIES FROM
OUR WOMBS AND DASH THEM ON THE ROCKS and
then we're gonna make them *get down on their kneeeessssss and
eat those babies up*

CONNIE
WE'RE GONNA CUT THEIR TONGUES OUT OF
THEIR STUPID FUCKIN HEADS AND THEN WE'RE
GONNA SKULL-FUCK THEM WHERE THEIR
TONGUE ONCE WAS

AMINA
GANDHI!

SOFIA
GANDHI!

ZUZU/MAEVE
GANDHI!

LUKE/CONNIE/ASHLEE
GANDHI!

ALL THE GIRLS
GANDHI'S UNITE! GANDHI'S DESTROY!

ASHLEE
WE ARE YOUR WORST NIGHTMARES AND WE'RE
COMING FOR YOU PHILADELPHIA

ALL THE GIRLS
ARGGGGGHHHHHH

ASHLEE
WE'RE COMING FOR YOU AKRON, OHIO

ALL THE GIRLS
ARGGGGGGGGGGGHHHHHHH

ASHLEE
WE'RE COMING FOR YOU LANOKA HARBOR,
NEW JERSEY!

ALL THE GIRLS
TAMPA
TAMPA
TAMPA
TAMPA
TAMPA
TAMPA
TAMPA
TAMPA
TAMPA
TAMPA
TAMPA
TAMPA
TAMPA
TAMPA
TAMPAAAAAAAAAARRRGHHHH

CONNIE
Luke. You coming with us?

LUKE
Yup!

SOFIA
It's show time

SOFIA reaches down her tights and gets a glob of period blood. She wipes it across her face like warpaint.

ASHLEE
You better frickin kill that solo, Zu

ZUZU
I will

MAN ON THE MIC
Girls you're up

ZUZU *(To herself.)*
I will. Or die

> *MUSIC! THE GIRLS strut onstage in their Citizen costumes – a weird, robotic little strut – bellies sucked in, beads of sweat on their forehead, stiff smiles across their faces.*
>
> *It begins. The Gandhi dance. CONNIE sits gracefully on the floor. THE GIRLS dance as Citizens around her. Everything seems to be going well – THE GIRLS are in sync, smiling. CONNIE looks radiant. SOFIA is slowly bleeding through her tights… It's almost time for the Spirit of Gandhi to break out and do her solo. ZUZU is pale and sweating. She gets slightly out of step with the Citizens. AMINA watches her out of the corner of her eye, concerned. ZUZU steps forward, determined, ready to launch into the frenzied, fever dream that is her "special part."*
>
> *She goes into her first twirl sequence and executes it brilliantly. She smiles.*
>
> *She flips across the stage – backwards aerial. She nails it. She's feeling good. She's feeling really good. She's dancing. She's not dancing – she's existing. She's in it. She's grooving. She is possessed. She kicks her leg with great force – it sails up above her head and slices past her ear. But something's off. She's off-balance. She's kicked*

her leg too hard. And her other leg – her supporting leg – slips out from under her like a bad leg on a chair. ZUZU falls. She bounces on her ass. She is stunned. She sits there for a half-second, totally overwhelmed.

ZUZU'S MOM *(From the audience.)*
Get up, get up, get up!

Everything slows down. We're watching the scene from outer space.

ZUZU looks up. Her face very pale. Her eyes glassy. Like a little wounded fawn that knows it's about to die and is too stunned to move.

ZUZU'S MOM *(From the audience.)*
She forgot it. Oh god, she forgot it

ZUZU is breathing so hard that we can see her rib cage go in-and-out, in-and-out.

ZUZU'S MOM *(Willing it.)*
Keep going!

Thunderous applause from the audience.

ZUZU'S MOM *(Slow-mo.)*
Keeeeeeep goooooooing!!!!!!!!

The entire audience joins in – huge, muffled, booming, slow-mo, space alien... is this even happening... They start chanting her name.

ZUZU'S MOM and THE AUDIENCE
ZUZU! ZUZU! ZUZU! ZUZU! ZUZU! ZUZU! ZUZU!

ZUZU looks at THE GIRLS. She's failed them. Their dreams of Tampa are dying...

AMINA looks at ZUZU frozen on the floor. She leaps out of line with the Citizens. The dance resumes like clockwork.

ZUZU lies there like she's dead. Like she has died. As if this were all part of the piece. ZUZU is death. And AMINA is God incarnate.

AMINA dances the part of the Spirit of Gandhi, dressed like a lowly Citizen. She is spectacular.

The dance is genuinely moving. Strong and in sync and full of emotion and life. It makes the audience cry.

The dance ends. There is rapturous applause. THE GIRLS exit, walking off-stage – their chests heaving, rib-cages showing…

CONNIE grabs AMINA by the arm.

CONNIE
What were you doing??????

AMINA
What're you talking about?!

CONNIE
You should've given her a chance!

AMINA
She choked!

CONNIE
For a split second! She would have made it

AMINA
She choked, Connie, *she choked*

CONNIE
You didn't even give her *a second* / to recover–

AMINA
She needed / help! I was saving the dance–

CONNIE
You just jumped in front of her

AMINA
No, I–

CONNIE
And she didn't / even have a second to recover

AMINA
She fell down!

CONNIE
To catch her breath

AMINA
You don't have a second
You don't
A second is too long
You hesitate. You're dead

CONNIE
…
…
You're such a jerk

AMINA
Connie, no, I–

CONNIE
IT WAS NOT YOUR PART!!!!

AMINA
I didn't do anything wrong!
I was just trying to help!
I just went off my instincts
I'm not going to apologize
For just *reacting*
I just–
I did it

CONNIE

…

AMINA

My body just–
I'm sorry
I would've waited for her
I would've waited for her forever
But
My body just–

…

It just *went*

12

In some forgotten corner of the auditorium...

ZUZU is still lying facedown on nasty-ass carpet like she were dead.
MAEVE sits beside her, holding her wolf cards.

MAEVE
Wanna see my wolf pack?

ZUZU doesn't respond.

MAEVE
They're called the Druids, that's their pack name
My mom paid $25 and now I get their pictures in the mail
...
...
I can track them online, too, it's pretty cool

ZUZU *(Into the carpet.)*
Cool

MAEVE
Yeah it's pretty cool

ZUZU
...
...
...
...
...
...
...
...
...
Hey Maeve

MAEVE
Yeah

ZUZU
What do you want to do with your life?

MAEVE
I don't know
Maybe astrophysics or something like that

ZUZU
Not dance?

MAEVE
Nah, I don't think so
…
…
I want to do something cosmic, you know
…
…
I mean, I know that dance can be kind of cosmic
But I mean like *actually* cosmic
Like stars or volcanoes or something
…
…
…

ZUZU
Yeah I want to do something cosmic, too

MAEVE
Like black holes
Are so scary
And cool

ZUZU
Yeah

MAEVE
Hey Zuzu

ZUZU
Yeah

MAEVE
Can I ask you a question?

ZUZU *(Still into the carpet.)*
Yeah

MAEVE
Have you ever flown?

ZUZU
…
…
…
In a plane?

MAEVE
No
Like
…
…
In a room

ZUZU
I don't think so

MAEVE
Oh

ZUZU
Have you?

MAEVE
I think I *have*
…
…
Like sometimes I concentrate on it
Really hard
And all of a sudden
I'm flying

ZUZU
In a room

MAEVE
Yeah

ZUZU
Like this one

MAEVE
It doesn't have to be like / this one

ZUZU
But any room

MAEVE
Yes

ZUZU
…

MAEVE
…

…

…

It sort of washes over me. Like sleep. Like all of a sudden I
notice my leg is falling asleep. And I feel it crawling up from the
bottom of my feet and I'm like: Uh-oh. I'm about to fly again.

…

…

And then I hold my breath and let my eyes go soft focus and
I try to concentrate on it but also I can't concentrate on it too
hard or else it goes away. I have to sort of concentrate on it
sideways, you know?

…

…

ZUZU
…

MAEVE

And then I just sort of float away. And I'm constantly in danger
of crashing to the ground if I don't keep my mind in the right
place. But if I *do*, if I do keep my mind in the right place then
I just sort of float to the top of the room and sit there

ZUZU

That's amazing

MAEVE

And sometimes when I'm at the top of stairs
My body just takes off
And I just glide down
Like I'm a ghost
And I always think
Oh my god
This is the end
I'm about to fall down the stairs and break my neck
But then I just float down and I'm fine

ZUZU

…

MAEVE

And one time I flew over the Great Lakes and then up
into Canada and over the Rocky Mountains? Maybe I was
dreaming. But I just went out the window. And I was flying
belly down over the mountains. Like right over the face of
them. And I saw all their crags and crevices and pockmarks
like I was looking into their faces. I don't know how I
could've seen the mountains' faces if I hadn't been actually
flying like that.

ZUZU

I've never flown before. Not even in my dreams. The only
thing like that that's ever happened to me is sometimes I wake
up and it feels like I'm falling through the bed

AMINA appears in the doorway, a giant crown on her head.

AMINA
Hey

MAEVE
Hey

ZUZU
…

MAEVE
Nice crown

AMINA
Oh, thanks

AMINA reaches up and tries to take it off. But it won't budge.

AMINA
It's stuck in my hair, I can't get it off

MAEVE
What's it for?

AMINA
I won the MVP Miss Dance of Tomorrow?

MAEVE
Really????

AMINA
Yeah……………………..

AMINA stops struggling with her crown.

MAEVE
What does that even *mean?*

She shrugs.

AMINA *(Apologizing.)*

It's a special award. For potential. Or something.

I guess I like… get to be fast-tracked to Tampa. I don't know…

(for the solo division)

MAEVE

You're going to Tampa?

She nods.

MAEVE

No matter what?

AMINA

I guess so

MAEVE

Cool

AMINA Looks at ZUZU lying facedown on the carpet.

AMINA

Is she okay?

MAEVE shrugs.

MAEVE

We're just talking

AMINA looks at ZUZU – a little scared. She lifts up the hood of her dance jacket and puts it over her head so that it covers her crown. She approaches ZUZU on the carpet.

AMINA

…

…

…

Zuzu?

…

…

…

I just wanted to check on you and make sure that you were okay
…
And make sure you knew
That everyone's so happy we won the group dance!
We're going to Akron!!!!!!! *Yayyyy!*
No one even cares that you fell down
They all thought it was supposed to happen
They thought it was *cool*
They thought it was really cool

…
…
Zu?
…
…
…
Are you mad at me?

Still with her face in the carpet…

ZUZU
I'm not mad I just can't really look at you right now…

AMINA
Um. That's okay…
Do you want me to like– sit with you? Or, I can get you some water??

ZUZU
…
…
…

MAEVE
I think she just needs some time and space

AMINA *(Smiling weakly.)*
Okay. No prob
…
…

…

Um, I guess I should…

…

…

She gives MAEVE a little wave.

AMINA
Bye Maeve

MAEVE
Bye

AMINA
Bye Zu

…

…

Nobody's mad, okay?

ZUZU

…

MAEVE

…

AMINA

…

AMINA exits.

ZUZU

…

…

…

…

…

…

Is she gone?

MAEVE
Yeah

> *ZUZU gets up. She looks like death. Her eyes are bloodshot. She wipes her eyes, the snot off her face. She splashes water on her face.*

MAEVE *(Suddenly self-conscious.)*
Hey Zu. Don't tell anyone I told you that.

ZUZU
Huh?

MAEVE
About the flying

ZUZU
Oh. I won't

MAEVE
I don't want people asking me questions

ZUZU
I won't tell, I promise

…

…

…

> *ZUZU looks in the mirror. She plays with her lips, her fangs.*

> **MAEVE**
> *And one day I'll forget that I ever used to fly. Because the truth is –*
> *I did. I did actually have the power to fly. Or to float, or whatever. But somehow, along the way I forgot about it. I forgot all about it. It was the coolest thing I ever did. And I forgot it. I forgot it ever happened. On multiple occasions. It happened. And I forgot.*

ZUZU *(Looking in the mirror.)*

.... Ugh. I wish I could throw up but I don't
think I can do it ....

....

...

...

...

...

...

Maeve?

MAEVE

Yeah?

ZUZU

You wanna know something?

MAEVE

Yes

ZUZU

I knew I was gonna fall before I fell
I don't know why
My leg just didn't work
And I knew it
Before it even stopped working
It's like I dreamed it
I don't know
...from past lives...
.......or future lives....
or something

MAEVE *(Smiling apologetically.)*

I'm sorry

ZUZU

It's fine

MAEVE

…

…

Hey Zuzu?

ZUZU
Yeah

MAEVE
I think I have to go find my mom now

ZUZU
That's fine

MAEVE
It's getting pretty late

…

…

Are you okay?

ZUZU
Yeah I'm fine.

MAEVE
Do you want me to find your mom?

ZUZU
No it's fine

She smiles at her.

ZUZU
I'm just gonna stay here for a minute and–

MAEVE
Okay

MAEVE runs out of the room and goes to find her mom. We see her run into her mother's arms.

MAEVE
Mom! We won!

MAEVE'S MOM
Yay!

> *ZUZU stands there – still smeared with face paint and blood from her arm. She closes her eyes. She holds her breath. She concentrates.*

> *She throws herself into the wall. She throws herself into the wall again.*

ZUZU
…
…
…
…
…
…
…
…
Ow

13

Night. ASHLEE and CONNIE are waiting outside to be picked up.
They have coats on over their tights and leotards. Their faces are
still painted bright, freakish colors.

Headlights. ASHLEE notices something…

ASHLEE
Connie

CONNIE
What?

ASHLEE
That man is looking at us

CONNIE looks. Then waves…

ASHLEE
Oh my god, he's waving back

CONNIE *(Calling out.)*
We're just waiting for her mom–

ASHLEE
Shh!

CONNIE *(Laughing.)*
He's probably wondering why we're not wearing any pants

ASHLEE

…

CONNIE

…

ASHLEE
Should I show him my leotard?

ASHLEE starts to unzip her jacket.

ASHLEE

Show him your horse

CONNIE pulls out her lucky horse. They show the man their horse and leotard. Then...

ASHLEE

Oh my god, he's coming over! Connie, Run! Connie, RUNNNNN!

They run away, shrieking.

...

   ...

      ...

         The moon comes out...

            ...

              ...

                ..   *A knock at the door.*

                .

                        SOFIA

                        Just a minute

                          SOFIA alone in the bathroom, scrubbing the blood out of her tights.

                          Another tentative knock.

                        SOFIA

I said, JUST A MINUTE. CAN I NOT HAVE TWO MINUTES PEACE WITHOUT SOMEONE INVADING ME ???!!!!!! JESUS CHRIST!

She feels deeply ashamed
for yelling.

SOFIA's MOM
Sofia, hunny, do you need
help in there?

SOFIA

…

…

…

…

…

…

Sorry, Mom. I'll be out in a minute

SOFIA's MOM
Because I can come in
and help you, if you want?

SOFIA

…

SOFIA's MOM
There are tampons under
the sink, and–

SOFIA
Mom!

SOFIA's MOM
Pads. If you want them
It might be easier to use a pad…
Just to start

…

…

Or you can use a tampon,
if you want to…
Do you know how to do it?

SOFIA
Mom, no. Stop

SOFIA's **MOM**
Okay, I'm not trying to–

…

…

Just sometimes it helps if
you get up on the counter
and look in the mirror

SOFIA
Mom, no

SOFIA's **MOM**
Just so you can see where
it goes

SOFIA
I'm not going to look at it

> *SOFIA is quietly weeping
> over her tights.*

SOFIA
*I don't want to look at it
I'm never going to look at it*

SOFIA's **MOM**
Okay, then don't look
Don't look then, hunny
Just put it in
It's just like you're giving
yourself a shot

SOFIA still weeping over her tights…

CONNIE appears in front of the moon, safe and sound…

CONNIE
Mom, I'm home!

*She goes into her bedroom and gets a box down off
a shelf. She slowly starts to unpack it. It's full
of horses.*

*AMINA on her stomach. A pillow between her legs. She prepares
herself – almost like she's talking herself through a number.*

AMINA
And I'm walking down a beach

…

…

And they've got their thumb tucked inside the back of my jeans
And I can feel the weight of their arm kind of pulling my jeans *down*

…

…

And then they lay me down
Onto the sand
And they take off my jeans…

…

…

…   *(She looks at the door for a second…*   Mom?

…

…   *Then gets up and locks it. She returns to her position*

…   *on the floor and starts to gently rock herself*

…   *back and forth.)*

…

And then they start to kiss my ankle

…

And then my calf…….

…

And then my knee……………

…

And then they start to pull my swimsuit *down*….

. . . . .

. . . .

. . .

. .

.

AMINA masturbates.

CONNIE with her horses under the moon.

SOFIA in the bathroom, still weeping and scrubbing her bloody tights.

(A triptych of girlhood.)

14

Afternoon. THE GIRLS climbing up the stairs to the dance studio…

SOFIA and ASHLEE sit in the dressing room drinking afternoon coffee. They're avoiding putting on their dance clothes. They pass one cup between them – taking dainty sips, taking turns…

The trophy from Philadelphia is there in a corner. It's four-feet tall.

AMINA enters. THE GIRLS look at each other – a little wary and tentative but ultimately everyone wanting to be supportive and kind…

AMINA
Hey

SOFIA/ASHLEE
Hey

AMINA
…We're going to Akron!…

SOFIA
…We're going to Akron!…

AMINA
Yayyyyy!

ASHLEE
We totally did it!

AMINA strokes the trophy.

AMINA
It's so big

SOFIA
They only get bigger…

AMINA
How are you guys doing?

SOFIA
Fine

ASHLEE
Fine

SOFIA
That's so cool about your thing, p.s.

AMINA	**ASHLEE**
Oh thanks	Yeah, Tampa! That's so cool

AMINA
Thanks, Ashlee

ASHLEE
I didn't even know that could happen!

AMINA
Me either

SOFIA
You're like *a star*, Amina

AMINA
Haha not really

SOFIA
No that's what everyone was saying. They were like: Wow.
She's such *a star*

AMINA
I don't know, I feel like I didn't even do that good, to be honest…
I was so rattled…

ASHLEE
No you were *really* good, Amina. It was amazing.
…
…
Are you going to do the special Gandhi part in Akron?

AMINA
I don't know

AMINA
…

SOFIA
…

ASHLEE
…

AMINA
…

SOFIA
It's not *bad*. It's not a *bad thing* to be the star

AMINA	**ASHLEE**
I know	She's not "the star." Dance Teacher Pat just likes her the best

SOFIA
And the judges! And all of western / Pennsylvania

AMINA
No, he doesn't!

ASHLEE
Yes, he does, Amina

SOFIA
Um, yeah, Amina, he totally does

AMINA
…

SOFIA
You don't have to lie about it

AMINA
I'm not lying

SOFIA
At least don't lie about it
At least *be honest*

AMINA
I still lose sometimes

SOFIA
Sometimes

AMINA
And it really sucks when I lose because there's a lot of
pressure on me. And it's really embarrassing
…
Like you guys lose all the time. Whatever
But if I lose, I'm like a perfectionist / and

ASHLEE
That's really mean

AMINA
What?

ASHLEE
You're being really mean

AMINA
I'm just being honest

SOFIA
No, actually, now you're being mean

AMINA
I'm just saying…
That the stakes *are higher* / for me

ASHLEE
Okay

AMINA
What? You said to be honest. I'm not allowed to be honest???

ASHLEE
Have fun with all your crowns

AMINA
What?

ASHLEE
I said: HAVE FUN WITH ALL YOUR CROWNS

…

…

…

INSTEAD OF FRIENDS

…

…

…

ALL YOU HAVE IS CROWNS

…

…

SO HAVE FUN WITH THEM

> *AMINA exits towards the dance studio. ZUZU is climbing up the stairs. She walks straight into the studio and approaches DANCE TEACHER PAT.*

ZUZU
I think I'm quitting dance

DANCE TEACHER PAT

…

…

…

You know, if you quit, you can never come back

ZUZU

I know

DANCE TEACHER PAT

I'm not just talking about logistics, Zuzu
I'm talking about *your body*
You are training your body right now
And if you quit
Your body will go through puberty and change
And it will be *impossible* for you
To get it back
You won't be able to change your mind

ZUZU

…

DANCE TEACHER PAT

Look at your mom
She was a really special dancer once
She could've done whatever she wanted
And now…

He shrugs.

DANCE TEACHER PAT

Is that what you want?

AMINA pokes her head into the studio.

AMINA

Oh, sorry!

She makes a beeline for the corner.

AMINA

I'm just warming up

DANCE TEACHER PAT leans down so he's eye level with ZUZU.

DANCE TEACHER PAT

Just don't make a decision you'll regret for the rest of your life

THE GIRLS sipping coffee in the dressing room...

SOFIA
Drinking black coffee makes me feel like a Mom

ASHLEE
Drinking black coffee makes me feel like a Cowboy

SOFIA looks at ASHLEE and grins.

SOFIA
Wanna make it magic?

She pulls out of fistful of sugar packets form her tracksuit and very carefully, almost ritualistically, empties them one-by-one into the coffee and stirs.

LUKE enters.

LUKE
Hey

SOFIA/ASHLEE
Hey

CONNIE enters.

CONNIE
Hey

SOFIA/ASHLEE
Hey

CONNIE
Have you guys seen Zuzu?

SOFIA
No

ASHLEE
No

CONNIE
Is she doing okay?

ZUZU comes in from the studio.

ZUZU
See you later

CONNIE   **SOFIA**
Where are you going?   Hi Zuzu

ASHLEE
Hi Zuzu

ZUZU
I'm taking the day off

LUKE
Wait. I'm coming with you

LUKE grabs his dance bag and scrambles after her.

ASHLEE
Bye Zu!

CONNIE watches SOFIA stirring the coffee.

CONNIE
What are you doing?

SOFIA grins at her.

SOFIA
I'm making it magic

AMINA dancing in the studio. DANCE TEACHER PAT watches her.

DANCE TEACHER PAT
Amina

AMINA
What?

DANCE TEACHER PAT
You're holding back

AMINA
No I'm not

DANCE TEACHER PAT
Don't worry about what's going on in the dressing room
Just dance
Unleash

AMINA
I *am* unleashing

DANCE TEACHER PAT
No you're not.
…
Where are your shoes?!

AMINA
I forgot my dance bag

DANCE TEACHER PAT
Amina

AMINA
What???

DANCE TEACHER PAT
What's going on with you?

AMINA
Nothing

> *She dances.*

DANCE TEACHER PAT
Stop

> *She does.*

DANCE TEACHER PAT
Look at me

She does.

DANCE TEACHER PAT
Where's the girl I saw this weekend, huh?

AMINA
…

DANCE TEACHER PAT
You forget her at home, too?

THE GIRLS still in the dressing room, drinking coffee, not getting dressed. ASHLEE puts her feet on top of the trophy.

ASHLEE
Life is weird. And hard

CONNIE
Yeah

ASHLEE
I know I should be excited that we won and stuff but I'm in such a bad mood

CONNIE
Yeah I don't even really wanna go to Akron

ASHLEE
Is it always going to be like this?

SOFIA
Like what?

ASHLEE
I don't know. Just…

…

I feel all this pain
Inside my chest

Like all these things are hurting me
And I'm like turning into this giant *scar*, you know what I'm saying?
But also I feel bad about everything I ever say and everything
I ever do…

SOFIA
Don't feel bad!

ASHLEE
I don't know why! I just do…

CONNIE
That's because you're a sensitive person, Ash
You're a thoughtful, sensitive person

ASHLEE
..
  ..
    ..
      ..
        no

SOFIA
I love Amina

ASHLEE
I love Amina, too

In the studio.

AMINA *(To DANCE TEACHER PAT.)*
Sometimes I think I want to lose
Like I actually think I want to lose
Like I close my eyes and I say:
God. It's okay, if I lose
I don't mind this time
Like I feel like I hurt people
Just by existing
Like just by me, just I– *living*

It hurts everyone else
And I think: Okay, *pleasssse*, just let me lose.......................
But then I get up on that stage
And they take the trophies out
And when they take the trophies out
It's like I get the taste of metal in my mouth
And all of a sudden, all I want is to win
I want to win so bad
I just like, *pray for it*

DANCE TEACHER PAT
I don't think you have to feel bad about that

AMINA
…
…
…
Dance Teacher Pat?

DANCE TEACHER PAT
Yes, Amina?

AMINA
I don't want to do the special Gandhi part in Akron. I want
Zuzu to do it

DANCE TEACHER PAT
…
…
…
Okay

AMINA
Are you mad at me?

DANCE TEACHER PAT
I'm not *mad*…

AMINA

…

DANCE TEACHER PAT

But if Zuzu has the solo in Akron, she's going to take it all the way to Nationals

AMINA

That's fine

DANCE TEACHER PAT

And that's where all the casting directors are going to be, and where we're gonna wanna put our best foot forward as a team

She nods.

DANCE TEACHER PAT

This is bigger than one dance, Amina. You girls are building your legacy. Who do you trust with that legacy? Anyone? Or the strongest dancer on the team

AMINA

The strongest dancer on the team

DANCE TEACHER PAT

And who is that?

AMINA

…

DANCE TEACHER PAT

Who is the strongest dancer on the team?

AMINA

I don't know

DANCE TEACHER PAT

You don't know?

AMINA

I think I probably am, I just– the other girls are really…

DANCE TEACHER PAT
If you were an impartial judge who didn't know anything about anyone, who came in here and watched you all dance. Who would you say deserved it?

AMINA
I don't know. I think Zuzu can / do it

DANCE TEACHER PAT
Why do you pretend not to know things you know?

AMINA
I don't know!!!

…

…

I think it's me

…

..

.

DANCE TEACHER PAT
Good. You'll do the solo, then

AMINA stands there bereft.

DANCE TEACHER
There's a thousand other girls out there just as talented as you, Amina, and they're *owning* it.

ZUZU and LUKE climbing up a hill, afternoon sunshine.

LUKE
Zuzu?

ZUZU
Yeah?

LUKE
Can I ask you a question?

ZUZU
Is it about dance?

LUKE
No

ZUZU
Then, shoot.

LUKE
How do you want to lose your virginity?

ZUZU
Uh–

LUKE
Like how do you want it to happen

ZUZU
Oh

LUKE
Do you know?

ZUZU
Oh. Yeah

LUKE
You do?

ZUZU
Oh yeah

LUKE
Will you tell me?

She looks at him.

ZUZU
Well there's two versions of the story.

LUKE

…

ZUZU

In one version I'm an enchantress. Like an enchantress,
enchantress. Like I'm actually an enchantress. (Don't tell
anyone this.) Like Lion, the Witch and the Wardrobe style.
Like somebody comes and gets me through the cupboard
and is like: Dude! You're an enchantress. And I go off into
this magical world. And I get to live whole lifetimes there as
a queen and an enchantress but then I can come back to earth
and no time has passed.

LUKE

…

ZUZU

So that's one version.

LUKE

Uh-huh

ZUZU

And the other is that I'm an enchantress in a movie

LUKE

Oh

ZUZU

And he's my

LUKE

Co-star

ZUZU

Leading man

LUKE

Cool

ZUZU

He's Canadian
I don't know why he's Canadian he's just always been Canadian
…
Theodore

LUKE

That's his name?

ZUZU

Yup. Theodore. I don't know why. I don't even like that name.
It just came to me

LUKE

In a dream?

ZUZU

I don't know. It just came.
And we fall in love

LUKE

How do you fall in love?

ZUZU

What?

LUKE

How does that happen? How do you fall in love?

ZUZU

We just are

LUKE

Automatically

ZUZU

Well not automatically…

LUKE

Both of you?

ZUZU
I think so?

LUKE
At the same time?

ZUZU
Yes

LUKE
But how do you *know*?

ZUZU
Um

LUKE
That you're in love. Like how does it *actually* happen?

ZUZU thinks.

ZUZU
I think it's just like we meet each other. And we feel like we've known each other before. Like in past lives. Like we're old souls when we're together and he's known me forever so falling in love is really just like remembering or like catching up to what we already were...you know?
…
Does that make sense?

LUKE shrugs.

LUKE
So what happens next in your story?

ZUZU
So anyway we fall in love and we get engaged and we buy an apartment. In New York City! And after we've bought our apartment–

LUKE
How old are you?

ZUZU

I don't know. Twenty-three?

So we go there one day – during the day, before we've moved in – just to you know plan out how we're going to lay out all the furniture in the house. And it's just a big empty apartment. And we get to decide where all the chairs go. And all the tables. And all the cups. And it's just like *bliss.* And he leads me through the apartment by my hands. And sunlight is streaming through the windows. And he lays me down on the floor – and it's a hardwood floor. And it's kinda warm because of all the sunlight. And my back is on the warm, hardwood floor. And we lose our virginities to each other. And as he, um, enters me. I open my eyes. And *he* opens *his* eyes. And this sounds *crazy* but our souls kind of touch through our eyes and like. Just for a moment. We become one being.

They sit on the grass.

LUKE

Are you guys married?

She shakes her head.

ZUZU

No, we're engaged

…

…

…

But then you know what's funny

Sometimes–

And not all the time

But sometimes–

I keep thinking for a little bit

And do you know what happens? In my mind?

LUKE

No

ZUZU
It's like five years later
(This is crazy)
But it's like five years later
And I have these two beautiful children
Two beautiful daughters
And he dies

LUKE
He dies?

ZUZU
Yeah. I don't know exactly how. Maybe a car crash. But he dies.
And we're like living in the country. The country outside of New
York City. With a trellis. And he dies. And I'm like this dancer
slash astrophysicist *widow* with these two beautiful babies. And
then one day someone comes to visit me. He drives all the way
to visit me. And when his car pulls up into my driveway, I go
outside to welcome him. And I've got like one baby on my hip.
And one baby by the hand. And I'm standing under the trellis.
Just saying: hello. And then I take him inside. And I make
him just the most beautiful lunch. Just the most beautiful lunch
you've ever seen. With like cheese. And olives. And beautiful
salads and things like that. And we sit on the floor. And the
babies fall asleep. And afterwards we drink coffee.

LUKE
That sounds nice

ZUZU
And do you know who that someone is????

LUKE
No?

ZUZU
It's Dance Teacher Pat.

She laughs and laughs.

ZUZU
Isn't that weird!

…

…

I don't know why it's him. But it is. It is.

ZUZU lies back in the grass. The sky, the breeze, the trees…

ZUZU
OH MY GOD

LUKE
What?

ZUZU
I just decided something

LUKE
What

ZUZU
THIS IS MY LAST DAY OF DANCE ON EARTH!!!!!!!

THE GIRLS in the dressing room. SOFIA has (finally) finished making the magic coffee.

SOFIA
Alright, it's ready. Who wants a sip?

CONNIE
I do

SOFIA
If you take a sip, you pledge your eternal allegiance to CZALMSA [z-alm-sah]

CONNIE
Zalm-wahhhh?

SOFIA
Our group! Connie, Zuzu, Ashlee, Luke, Maeve, Sofia and Amina. *(Sounding it out.)* C – Z – A – L – M – S – A

CONNIE
But there's no "c" in ZALMSA!

SOFIA
The "c" is silent. Like in czar

CONNIE
Oh.

ASHLEE
We could be Zalm-sakkkkkkk

SOFIA
CZALMSA's cooler

CONNIE
…

SOFIA
Trust me, Connie. It's cool to be the silent "c"

CONNIE
Yeah…

SOFIA
You're like our secret weapon

CONNIE
I think I'm just tired of being a secret…

| **SOFIA** | **ASHLEE** |
| How are you a secret? | No! |

CONNIE
I don't know. I just feel like I am

ASHLEE
You're not a / secret

SOFIA
We can be Zalmsakkk, then. We can totally be ZALMSAC

SOFIA gives them a devilish look, then takes a sip of the magic coffee.

SOFIA
I solemnly swear my eternal allegiance................ to ZALMSAC

She hands the coffee to CONNIE. CONNIE takes a sip. It's really sweet.

CONNIE
Oof

…

…

To ZALMSAC

ASHLEE takes a sip.

ASHLEE
ZALMSAC

…

…

…

It kind of sounds like an anti-depressant

SOFIA
Huh?

ASHLEE
Like those commercials? Feeling worthless? Take Zalmsac

SOFIA
That's Zoloft

ASHLEE
No but in general. It sounds like that

CONNIE
My mom takes anti-depressants and she says I'm probably
going to have to, too

ASHLEE
Well, now you won't have to because you can just take Zalmsac

CONNIE
Thanks

ASHLEE
Here I'm going to give you a little bit of Zalmsac right now

She sticks her fingers under her armpit to collect sweat.

ASHLEE
Sofia?

ASHLEE sticks her fingers under SOFIA's armpit, too.

ASHLEE
Okay. Then you just apply the Zalmsac to the upper lip…

ASHLEE dabs the sweat on CONNIE's upper lip.

CONNIE
Thank you.

ASHLEE blows on CONNIE's upper lip. She kisses her on the mouth.

ASHLEE
And then you'll feel better, soon.

CONNIE takes ASHLEE's hand.

CONNIE

*And in twenty years, you will sit in my
apartment while you're on a business trip in
New York City, and I will tell you that I've
spent the fall trying not to kill myself,
and you will tell me that you spent all of high
school trying not to kill yourself. You will tell
me how you got on a bus, and found a doctor,
and rode the bus to the doctor, and begged
the doctor not to call your parents, and went
on anti-depressants at the age of fourteen,
and all this time, I was walking by you,
all this time our bodies were sharing spaces,*

135

> and I had no idea. And we will sit on the floor
> and drink wine and cry the same way we cry
> in banks and on airplanes and in all sorts of
> public places — quietly and full of shame but
> grateful to be quiet and shameful together —
> and we will talk about our jobs and the people
> we are dating, and suddenly, for the first time
> in years, I will believe in fate. That somehow all
> of this was pre-determined. You and me sitting
> here now. You and me sitting there then.
> I always knew there was something
> about us that was the same.

SOFIA
I want some, too.

ASHLEE dabs a little sweat on SOFIA's upper lip.

MAEVE enters.

MAEVE
Hey guys!

ASHLEE/CONNIE	**SOFIA**
Hey!	Maeve! Get over here

MAEVE
I'm late!

SOFIA
It doesn't matter. Sit down.

She does.

SOFIA
Drink this

SOFIA hands MAEVE the coffee.

MAEVE
What is it?

SOFIA
It's a potion

CONNIE
It's a spell

ASHLEE
It's just coffee

MAEVE
It hurts my teeth

CONNIE
Guys, it's 4:07. Should we go in?

They all look towards the door.

ASHLEE
Let him come and get us

They huddle in a circle – the magic coffee in the middle like a cauldron.

SOFIA
Girls? I have to tell you something that happened to me yesterday but you have to swear yourselves to secrecy.

ASHLEE
Zalmsac

CONNIE
Zalmsac

MAEVE *(Whispering.)*
I can feel it working on me

ASHLEE *(Whispering.)*
What?

MAEVE *(Whispering.)*
The potion

SOFIA
Late last night, in my bathroom…

After my mom went to sleep
I climbed up on the counter
And I pulled up my nightgown
And I *looked*

CONNIE
At what?

SOFIA
Everything

    The earth starts to shake.

SOFIA
And even though
It was the first pussy
That I ever, ever saw

SOFIA & **ASHLEE**
I knew *in my bones*
That no one could have
A pussy as perfect as mine

SOFIA & **ASHLEE** & **MAEVE** & **CONNIE**
And surely a person
With such perfect genitals
Is destined for greatness
It's written in the stars

    ZUZU joins the chant from her spot on the hill.

SOFIA & **ASHLEE** & **MAEVE** & **CONNIE** & **ZUZU**
And here's the thing about pussies
That they never, ever tell you
They're ageless! They're ageless!
Don't listen to their lies

    LUKE joins the chant from his spot on the hill.

SOFIA & ASHLEE & MAEVE & CONNIE & ZUZU & LUKE
My pussy is perfect
And it'll stay that way FOREVER

> *THE MOMS appears and chants with them.*

SOFIA & ASHLEE & MAEVE & CONNIE & ZUZU & LUKE
& THE MOMS *(Ecstatic!)*
I'll never forget
The day I first saw it
My perfect, perfect pussy

> *And DANCE TEACHER PAT!*

SOFIA & ASHLEE & MAEVE & CONNIE & ZUZU & LUKE
& THE MOMS & DANCE TEACHER PAT *(Utter ecstasy!)*
I knew *in my bones*
That no one could have
A pussy as perfect as mine
And surely a person
With such perfect genitals
Is destined for greatness
It's written in the stars
I wish that my *body*
Were as perfect as my pussy
I wish that my *face*
Were as perfect as my pussy

I wish that my *soul*
Were as perfect as my pussy
I wish that my *soul!*
Were as perfect as my pussy!
I wish that my *soul!*
Were as perfect as my pussy
I wish that my *soul!*
Were as perfect as my pussy!
I wish that my *soul* were as

perfect!

perfect!

perfect!

Prrrrrrrrrr
rrrrrrrrrr
rrrrrrrrrr
ruhhh!

AMINA dances, she dances, she dances. She is a tiny whirling dot.

AMINA
I'm gonna win
I'm gonna win
I'm gonna win
Not because of *you*
I am going to do it myself
Over the years
I will watch
As others fall away
Give up
Lose courage
I will keep going
Something will tell me to keep going
I will fail at first
But I will keep going
People won't like me
And other people will be better than me
But I will keep going
And then one day
The tide will start to turn
Inevitable
Unstoppable
Like the leaves falling off the trees
Winter is coming
And I am The Winter
You cannot deny me
My entire life will be a victory
And when they ask me how I did it I will say:
That I didn't listen to anyone
I had no teachers
No mentors
No parents
I am thankful for *nothing*
But myself
I rode the wave–

For eleven years
...twelve years
...thirteen years
I rode the wave–
For twenty years
...twenty-one years
...twenty-five years
I rode the wave–
For thirty years
...forty years
...fifty...
I rode the wave
Like I always knew how to ride the wave
And others kept falling along the way
But I kept riding
Til I was alone

   ...

I was alone

   ...

I was alone

   ...
   ...
   ..
   .

AMINA dancing. She is athletic, vicious, stunning. She absolutely dominates. She turns out to us. She hisses. She gnashes her fangs.

End of play.

WWW.OBERONBOOKS.COM